ORIGINATED SELF

How to develop self-love and inner happiness

SHANTINIQUE JAMES

FIRST EDITION

This is a work of creative nonfiction. Some parts have been fictionalized in varying degrees, for various purposes.

Edited by Ameesha Green

ISBN: 9781794025790 (paperback)

"You are the light of the world. A town built on a hill cannot be hidden. Neither do people light a lamp and put it under a bowl. Instead they put it on its stand, and it gives light to everyone in the house. In the same way, let your light shine before others, that they may see your good deeds and glorify your father in heaven."

Matthew 5:14-16

This book is dedicated to my beautiful daughters Maliya and Ayla James, and to the people I love, especially my mother Charmece Bass. I would like to thank you so much for all your encouragement and support in my life.

To my loving husband Anthony, I want to say thanks for your motivation and continued support throughout our life together.

Contents

INTRODUCTION

This book is for people who believe in a higher power (God, the Universe, or Source) and are struggling to overcome certain situations. Life is like a story that is continuing to unfold. Have you ever come to a place in life where you just weren't satisfied? What about a time when you were wondering what your purpose is in life? Did these emotions race through your mind and cause you to have a breakdown?

I'm not sure on the specifics about how it happened for you, but I do know it happens. You're just living your "normal" life, and one day everything changes. You no longer want to do the job you've been working at, and suddenly realize you're just not happy in life or about yourself. These feelings bring you to a place of uncertainty and confusion about where to turn to. At times, these moments can make you feel lonely, conflicted, and weak.

There are so many circumstances in life that can overwhelm us, and this can affect us mentally, physically, and emotionally. If we can think about the powerful effect that positive changes can have on us, it should be critical to differentiate what's important in life compared to what's not. We will decide what is positive compared to negative.

So often, our life becomes this cycle of consistent behaviors and results that were not part of our plan. You may have seen your life going in a different direction, but you made other decisions and things changed. There is so much to focus on in the world that it can be easy to lose yourself. Losing your dreams and desires because you feel obligated to other people, work, and maintaining your daily life.

It can be hard to define what self-love or inner happiness is when you haven't personally experienced it. However, I do believe that every person can diagnose their happiness level when asked. If I asked you "Are you happy?" there should be a simple answer provided of yes or no, and not based on conditions or circumstances.

Happiness is not defined by what you have or who you are to other people. It is defined by how we feel about ourselves and our lives. Throughout life, we develop the routine of living on autopilot. This is when you wake up daily to the same routine and forget to become conscious about your decisions.

You are reacting to everything and every person that comes across your way. Reacting is normal, but when you are not conscious of your decisions, it can be dangerous. Being conscious of your decisions is simply making those deliberate decisions, and not allowing the moment to get the best of you.

For example, if you're driving to work and someone cuts you off, it makes you so upset you curse at them through the window. Keep in mind that they can't hear you, but it made you so mad that you just had to do it. You're also running late for work, therefore everyone at work is going to feel your wrath if they come off the wrong way. The point is that we repeat these daily actions without assessing them. And we live in a repetitive cycle of the life we believe to be ours. We choose this repetition over our happiness in an unconscious decision.

The purpose of "Originated Self" is to help you find your inner happiness and develop self-love. Considering life can grab a tight grip on you, it is crucial to develop strong care for yourself and have a shield. "Originated" means being created new or from something. "Originated self" is in every section of the book, because you are creating your overall self in every aspect of your life.

We are created by all the parts of us, and this hereby makes us whole. Every piece contributes to the self that becomes created. "Originated" has such a powerful meaning, such as "specific beginning", "create", "develop", and every word you can think of that signifies becoming who you are. This word is the best way to describe the meaning of one's self. It breaks down all the elements of life and who we can become as a person.

In order to develop self-love and inner happiness, you must understand the critical elements of life and yourself first. In this book, I will explain the different versions of 'Self' broken down by the important elements of a story. In a story, the most important elements are character, setting, plot, conflict, theme, and resolution.

I chose this method because when you take a moment to think about life, describing it as a story is an exciting way to do so. Your life is like a book that is continuously unfolding, and you have the power to write the story. Writing your own story helps you to navigate through the conflicts and the major plot, so you can develop resolutions that last.

The Character section talks about the *"Roleplay Self"* and this is the part of you that must participate with the world. When you are a character, it is not who you are daily, but can sometimes appear as if you are playing a role.

The Setting section talks about the *"Past, present, and Future Self"* and this is the part of you that reacts to what moment you're currently thinking of. Our brain has the capability to recall memories that are not in the moment and think thoughts that have not physically appeared. When we think about the past/future, we are living in that moment because we are completely blocking what's happening NOW and focusing on another time.

The Plot section talks about the *"Outer Self"* and this is your perspective on who you are and your life. We all feel that we should be a certain way, and this could be defined simply as focusing on how you look. You put this perspective on your life and make requirements of yourself for this world experience.

The Conflict section talks about the *"Inner Self"* and this is the part of you on the inside (the soul, the spirit). This section is about being more than this human body. Many people have different beliefs about whether we have a soul or spirit, but it's important to address your beliefs head on. Addressing your beliefs will allow you to understand what may be conflicting you in life and causing any unhappiness.

The Theme section talks about the *"In-between Self"* and this is the part of you that is involved in a faith practice or not (Christian, Buddhist, Atheist, etc...).

Lastly, the Resolution section talks about the *"Originated Self"*, which is the result of all the other versions of self. This is the core of the book and will provide overall guidance on how to develop self-love and inner happiness. By accepting and understanding who you are, you can create the life you love and dream about.

This message is best explained in the format of a story to ensure all the essential elements of the self are covered. When you understand each section, it can help you to break down all the parts of your life and see how you can improve them to develop self-love and inner happiness.

Each section will discuss life examples and from that, give you guidance on how to develop self-love and inner happiness. At the end of each section, you'll find the ***Extra motivation just for you!* (Notes from my personal journal)** portion. You'll see why in the "Why I wrote this book" section.

This book is personal to me because I too had been lost in life and confused about the next steps to take. I was emotionally hurt due to financial problems, relationships, faith, and more. All the factors that I thought were so important to me had the power to break me down in any moment, and that hurt.

It appeared that I was battling daily for my happiness. Whether someone said something to hurt me at work or I was sad about a disagreement with a family member. Despite what the problem was, I could not blame anyone for my unhappiness and lack of self-love. After I discovered what was affecting me, I started to grow in different areas of life due to methods I learned. These practices affected me in a positive way, and my goal is to share these methods with you, and with the world.

"This book was created as a guide to provide helpful ideas and techniques on how to develop self-love and inner happiness. I am not a certified therapist or counselor, and the concepts discussed in this book should not be considered of that. If you experience any mental health condition, I recommend seeing a therapist or mental health specialist."

WHY I WROTE THIS BOOK

Ever since childhood I've always had big dreams for life, and my dreams mostly involved helping others. I remember there was this compassionate, sweet, and emotional side to me that I just didn't understand. I grew up with a single mom and four other siblings, my sister Haeley and my three brothers Jimmy, Martel, and Elijah.

My mother always worked hard to make sure we had a home and food to eat because we were her main priority. I am forever grateful for the love she consistently provided and still does today. Growing up, sometimes I saw her cry, but I didn't really know why or what was happening to provoke her emotions. I only knew that in those moments, my main goal was to do what I could to stop her pain.

My heart has always been very empathetic. At a young age, I was unaware that this was an ability, and that I could help people heal. At the young age of 10, I began to write songs with the dreams of becoming a singer.

As I grew, writing songs ceased, but most importantly I started to write thoughts from my mind and what I was feeling. From the expression of myself through words, I was able to put it all on paper and compile many notes. These notes were stored for years as I wrote them, and they traveled with me wherever I went. The notes grew out of sadness, happiness, confusion, joy, love, peace, and understanding, but mostly out of growth.

After every section, this book gives you an open door to some very important notes I've personally wrote over the years. The reason I decided to include these notes is because my spirit lead me to.

When I reached 19, my life started to change, but it really changed at age 25. At this time, I learned the difference between being apart of a religion and having faith. Before this point in life, I thought I had faith, and that I knew all I could know in life or about the world. But this was not true. I discovered my true purpose and became very spiritual and remain spiritual until this day.

My life has always been and will forever be dedicated to helping others. This book includes a reflection on some of my past notes that helped me through painful days and nights, but also through the joyful periods.

Reading these notes years later helped me to see the wisdom within me, and at times I would help myself with my own words. The notes you read in this book will provide insight on life, the good, the bad, spiritual life, God (supreme being, creator of the universe), pain within, growth within, knowledge, and whatever your perception of the notes may be.

During my early teens, I didn't fully know what I was doing in life other than the fact that I wanted to have a general career such as a lawyer or teacher, but the spirit within kept calling me to WAKE UP and do things that made me happy, not for money. Life was calling me to become the best version of myself and stop allowing the world to define my life.

I am no longer the person who isn't happy and not following their dreams. I breathe in and out the happiness of following my dreams and inspiring others to become their best version of themselves.

Remember: Life is ever flowing, and you will always be growing. Where you are now is not where you'll be, but if you open your eyes, you'll enjoy the journey!

WITHIN THE DEEPEST

There's something waiting to burst from the shadows of the darkness and it's you.

All this conditioning and confusion is not.

Look within because you know that's where it's at.

You ask yourself over and over the things you know to be true, waiting for a moment of proof.

Alas the proof! It was already within you.

Your spirit cries "get me out", "let me breathe", "I can't stay another day in this prison you see!" But do you listen?

Confused by the thoughts of the world but aware of the knowing of your heart and soul.

When will you let go? Be free and run like the squirrels in the tree.

This life is yours, and fear is not. It's not who you are.

You know this, and you can't tell me you do not.

The soul calls out to you daily, moment by moment, asking for a chance in this real love romance.

But you reject. Afraid. Will this hurt? Will I fail? Questions that won't make a sinking ship sail.

Your heart is pure and all-knowing,

let the creative waters flow in.

In the silence we peak as our souls take a leap.

The chance they once longed for is finally here.

No more hiding in the shadows attempting to disappear.

The spirit calls so pick up the phone if you're still breathing, you are for sure home.

A MOMENT OF SILENCE

"Self-Actualization Technique"

In order to fully grasp the concept of this book, I have created some questions for you to ponder on.

The reason these questions are pertinent before reading the book is because they help you to understand where you are mentally, emotionally, physically, and spiritually.

When I "self-help" myself, it always involves asking the hard questions and answering them.

We must communicate with ourselves effectively in order to learn how to do it with others.

- Please write these questions down and take a moment to answer them.

- It is best to go someplace alone and have a moment of silence, so you can connect fully with yourself without distractions.

- Once you have answered them, you can put them aside until you have finished reading the book.

- When you have completed the book, come back to the questions and make some plans to act for the best.

1. Which area of life are you having trouble with?

2. Are you affected emotionally, physically, mentally, or all?

3. Are you currently living the life you want?

4. Are you happy with yourself and the decisions you make?

5. Are you at peace with certain aspects of life?

6. What do you need help with?

7. How's your health?

8. What do you do for fun?

9. What's your passion?

10. How much success have you experienced in your life from your perspective?

11. Is it important for you to have family and friends around?

12. How important is money?

13. How important is love?

14. On a scale of 1-10, how happy are you?

15. Do you trust your belief system?

16. What changes would you like to make as a result of this book?

Take a moment and journal your thoughts after you've answered these questions. If there is something I have not covered with these questions, then write it down.

Only you can understand what questions are in your heart. On that note, let's dive into "Originated Self".

ROLEPLAY SELF: CHARACTER

LIFE:

ROLEPLAY SELF is defined as the character you play in this world. I am not stating that life is only a game. But I would like you to take a moment and view it from the perspective of a story, movie, or game. When you allow yourself to view your life differently, it can help you make more objective decisions that could be beneficial.

The *roleplay self* consists of all worldly activities such as hobbies, career, finances, material possessions, community, daily activities with family and friends, social media, and more. "Worldly" is defined as anything created by and in this world vs life after death (the spiritual world). This is the part of you that must interact with the world or your daily life.

Besides, we couldn't just live in our house every day for the rest of our lives. We'd have to go out into the world eventually, whether it's to eat, purchase items, pay bills, or make money. While living on this earth, we cannot escape the fact that we must interact with the world.

There is a part of you that's completely different in each of these environments. When you go to work, school, parties, restaurants, and more, you will place yourself in the proper character for each activity. You can't act the same when you go to a party as when you're at work. There is a time and place for everything.

Therefore, you play these character roles just to participate and seem part of the scene. When I started to understand that most activities I participated in were created and controlled by someone, the first thing I wanted to do was stay at home all day. It was like a blow to the face. Suddenly, I realized that we are all humans attempting to take the same path and become creators. But what we created and offered to the world was our control.

Imagine understanding that EVERYTHING you use, watch, touch, and live by is created by a human just like you. This may sound crazy, but just hear me out. EVERYTHING that has ever been created is being controlled by someone. The jobs you work, TV, money, school, food, seriously everything. I'm not saying that this is a bad thing, but it is a bad thing when you don't know that you are one of those creators.

Why do they get to have all the fun? Can't we create too? Well, the answer to that question is yes and that's why I wrote this book for you.

It helps you recognize the parts of you that may have been affected by someone else's control in their story that they're creating. Roleplay self is just a role. Don't let it take over the real you that's inside. The you that stands up for what you want and dreams big. The you that is extremely happy with your decisions and madly in love with yourself.

How do we start this part of life and become this character you ask? Well let's get started on the journey of creation. We enter this world as a tiny, little infant and are at the beginning stage of life. This is the start of everything that we will experience on this earth.

As a baby, you are controlled and monitored by your parents 24/7. What your parents experience you do as well. Your level of influence on your life is non-existent, and this is just how it goes. As an infant, you are this free-from-fear born individual looking to start life here on earth and grow to become older. The only purpose at this age is to live, breathe, eat, and maybe bring joy to the one who is holding you.

Of course, no one can ever determine what's happening in the mind of an infant. **You are who your parents make you at this stage.** Your character in the world has not developed yet, other than being a precious little human.

After infancy, we enter the stage of toddlerhood. Although we can understand the child's language and personality a little more, it is still not apparent who they are or who they will become. **At this stage, you are still controlled by your parents and monitored.** You begin to learn new things like walking and talking.

Tasty foods become a major part of your journey, and you just can't get enough of them. Your little heart is so pure despite any living situations your parents may have put you in. Yet still, your character in the world has not fully developed and to everyone in the world you are this innocent little kid who is unaware of his/her decisions.

Toddlerhood was fun but watch out, now we're in middle childhood "a little kid". At this point, we start to think and use our minds for decisions, although it may not be consistent with the rest of the world. We start to develop a personality of our own and learn to like new things.

We now face difficult challenges that could affect us emotionally. We now know when mom and dad are not on a good page or why we can't get that toy we've always wanted. Life begins and the journey starts because we are conscious enough to bring awareness to it. We start to ask more questions and wonder about the things we see, and what we haven't seen before. Guess what? **Your character in the world still has not developed yet, and everyone is making their assumptions of how they think you will turn out.**

The next fun stage is adolescence, or as we call it "a young person". You may have different titles for the name of this stage, which is right before early adulthood. **Our personalities have**

developed, and our character is starting to develop. You're doing more things now, which allows you to participate with the world more often. You're in school, and at this place you must become an independent person who forces you to separate from your parents.

Of course, you or someone you know may have gone to school before this time, but this is when the experiences start to sink in. They have the power to influence the role you will play in this world, but most importantly to the *Originated Self* that you will become.

Thoughts are forming in your mind that can sometimes be good and sometimes bad. You start to think about who you want to be and what you want to do when you grow up. You have the pressure from all the others to determine what you want to do in life.

At home, you have responsibilities that teach you to have some independency. Life has started to meet you were you are and now you are conscious of it.

Early adulthood is the next stage, and you are now developing your character in the world more than ever. With the internet being so popular, there are so many different options for your future. Life has now developed in a way that you are able to take a stand for the things you want, although your parents might disagree.

This is a critical stage in life because it's when you become more developed into who you are and who you'll become. You may have had experiences that affected you in a positive or negative way. At this point, you'll begin to display the character traits provided to you from your environment, family, friends, decisions, entertainment, and more.

You start to become who you think you are, with uncertainty of who you are. Life can be hard or easy for you at this point, but it depends on your upbringing. What did your parents teach you? Did they help you learn how to live a stable life or the fundamentals of money? It's time for you to use what you've learned to develop the character that you will be.

Now, you may have had parents who taught you about life in a way that you feel completely prepared OR NOT. But who is ever *really* prepared? Honestly, you can only learn about life through your own experiences. No one can tell you how to live it or how it will be. **At this stage, the best thing to do is to start to develop a character from your heart's desires.** Your heart will lead you in the direction you need to go, whether you understand the process or not.

We then reach middle adulthood and at this stage, life is a result of the decisions we have made despite what our life has been. We have the power to make our own decisions and determine where our life will go. Our finances are affected, and our happiness, relationship, love of self, and more. **At this stage, we should have some idea as to who we are and what we are doing in the world.**

You are probably working a job you like/dislike, in a relationship you like/dislike, and living the way you like/dislike. This should be the time to enjoy yourself because you are so in love with who you are. You have made all the decisions needed to become who you need to be in this world and should be prepared for late adulthood, which is when you will relax.

The people around you or who know you have an idea of who you are and your role in the world. Your character "roleplay self" has now begun. At this point in life, we are often settled into the decisions that we think, or previously thought, were good for us. When you reach middle adulthood, you should have experienced the critical elements of life and fully decided where your path is going. Although you have been playing a role most of your adulthood, this is the time when your character sets in.

Late adulthood should be bliss compared to all the past events in life. Your place in this world and within your self should be more developed at this point. Because when you are in late adulthood, a lot of things change mentally, physically, and emotionally. You don't have the strength to do the things you could do when you were younger. This is not a bad thing; it's just something you should accept.

Late adulthood is finally here and what's happening in your life? It's normally a result of all the decisions you've made when you were in the previous stages. If you're at this stage and life isn't what you want it to be, I need you to know that's okay, because it's never too late.

Every day that you are alive can become a new day for you to make a change. The best thing for you to do at this stage is relax and enjoy having made it through life all these years, because some people haven't. But YOU did.

If you can, please take a moment and congratulate yourself, because life always has a stage where it gets challenging and hard to continue. I'm not sure how your finances, emotions, family, and life is right now or whether you're happy or not. **But I do want you to understand that NOW is the time to fully let go of everything and live life by getting into a more relaxed state of mind.** You can do this by telling yourself to accept the things you cannot change, and by understanding that you need to put your happiness and peace first.

As we grow, there are so many experiences that we will encounter. **These experiences become the originated version of our lives, and ultimately, they determine our day to day activities.** As we grow through the stages and ages, life becomes more of a reality and less of a dream.

When you were a little kid, everything in the world seemed as if it was right in the palm of your hands, but one day you realized that maybe that isn't the truth. There's something about this BIG world that seems to make us put a mask on the greater parts of ourselves to hide it. It's true that everything started from something, so maybe the people who first started the ways of living were afraid of who they truly were.

You and so many people all over the world are playing these roles that do not amount to half of who you truly are in your heart. Life makes you put these "filters" on because of the fear of exposing who you truly are. You're concerned with whether the world will like who you are underneath the mask. But I ask you: do you like who you are underneath the mask? *You should.*

We have no control over the environments we are put in as a baby, child, and teenager. And unfortunately, whether positive or negative, it does have the power to affect our overall life. The one power we do have is the ability to decide how we feel on the inside about ourselves and our life.

No one can take away our inside mind, body, or spirit. The world may try to use manipulative techniques to control you, but overall you can reject anything that doesn't make you happy. When I say "the world" I'm referring to countless amounts of other people who also have a lack of self-love and happiness, so they project it on everyone else.

The only difference is that some of these people have fame or popularity, so when they project their hurt, they put it in movies, cartoons, commercials, music, and more. What happens is they forget that there are other hurt people listening and looking for a way to grow, and that they should promote positive change vs negative.

For some reason, we fail at becoming who we truly want to be deep within. Deep within are the feelings of who you truly know yourself to be. It's easy to hide our innermost desires, because they don't always align with others'. We may appear not "normal" or seem weird for being different. But really, who is the same? I am not you and you are not me. We can never be each other, but we can always make sure we compare our experience and decisions to someone else's. How can you do this if you've never been anyone else?

Now, don't get me wrong, there are situations we experience that are similar. Having these similar situations allows us to have sympathy and empathy for one another. You just must remember that despite our similarities, we are all unique in our own way. This uniqueness is meant to help contribute to one another. What I lack, you may perfect. We can help each other out by being different, not the same. Your differentness in this world is beauty and you must accept that truth.

There are certain criteria that constitute the "Roleplay Self", which is your character in the world. These areas are very important to pay attention to, because they contribute to your overall experience here on planet earth.

As you grow, becoming a child to an adult, you are taught to act a certain way, with a certain manner, depending on your background or culture. In your case, maybe it was something your parents forced on you or maybe they forced some things and not others. Either way, you grew to develop this method to how you should live life.

A certain structure that you must abide by in order to live in the world. It became who you are, and who the entire essence of you were in the world. It's not that it was your intention to become this way, but there are some things we cannot avoid. The world is a busy place; it can grab a giant hold of you and take you into a place you will never understand. With all its creativity, growth, and expansion, it can be hard to hold on to the most important things in life.

Let's talk about how the "Roleplay Self" is associated with the "Originated Self". Now, we're going to look at a lot of things and I need you to follow along, so they make sense in end. When you are old enough to begin life on your own and start to make decisions yourself, this is when the journey begins. You must utilize all the skills, techniques, methods, and everything else that you were taught in order to navigate through life.

Although you have spent a short amount of time getting prepared for what you think is ahead, you have no idea that the world has been waiting on you all along. The world is a place with endless opportunities. So how about you come on a journey with me thorough a proto-life?

Suddenly, you're 19 years old and beginning to think more about life and where you want to go. You think about your career, friends, job, money, and everything under the moon. You're going to public school/private school and starting to develop an idea for your future. Maybe you'll become an actor or a lawyer?

You think to yourself about all of these great ideas and who you want to become. While watching a TV show, you admire all the actors who are doing such an excellent job. Well, maybe I'll become an actor, you think? You acknowledge the fact that the decisions you make now can affect your future, so you better choose wisely.

Maybe you had great guidance growing up, someone who taught you how to get your finances together or hang around the right people. Either way, the objective is to understand that now is the time to play the role you have been waiting to play since childhood. Every child dreams of driving a car before they can, and I know from my experience when I started to drive, it wasn't what it looked like all those years before.

So, you finally get your first job, and you're so excited about it. Now you can make your own money and have some independency. There's no one to tell you what to do anymore, because you make the rules for your life. Right? At least that's what we think until we realize our boss will tell us what to do too.

I'm not sure whether your first job was one of your dreams, but if so, I am completely jealous (just kidding)! After some time working at your job, you feel it's time to upgrade, maybe get some more money. If this company isn't going to give you a raise or promotion, then it's time to look somewhere else for work. You begin your job search to find something more feasible, because now you have bills to pay.

Life is becoming such a drag, and it's not the journey you imagined. That dream you once had of being an actor has slowly faded away, because working every day at the job you dislike/like is taking away the time you need to start planning for your career. As time passes, other things happen like building new relationships and having children, pushing your dreams further away than they've ever been.

One day, sitting alone, you ask yourself "Am I really happy?" and you know the answer. It's NO. For some reason although you know you're not happy, you can't figure out why, and why all a sudden, the rush of this has happened. You thought you were okay because you were at least getting by. Wasn't getting by enough because you knew that one day your dreams would come true? But one day you realized that day was never going to come if you didn't act on it.

This was the role you thought you had to play, because that's how all the others were playing. But that wasn't the truth for your life. It wasn't the way you had to live, but you were afraid because what you were doing was the most comfortable, considering it's all you've ever known. You've never seen anyone around you become an actor, so why would you believe you can? Yet, still there's something inside you saying *you can, and you will succeed no matter what.*

Actors can easily get into character and change roles, therefore it's time you did that for your personal life. So, you finally decide that you will take the leap and go to acting school despite any fears you have. From here on, you are now on the path you wanted in the first place.

You took the chance that you once feared, and it changed your life forever. The role you play in the world is now defined by you and not others. Every day, you wake up as this budding entrepreneur with excitement. Following your heart has made you love yourself extremely.

When you reflect on your past decisions, you're happy for your experiences because they've helped you form the *Originated Self* that you have become.

You can't help but imagine that if you never took that chance, where you would be? The character you're playing in your story is the one who makes people smile because of the ending. For the rest of your life, you will understand that your happiness should come first, and to follow your heart's desires.

Every day, you're determined to change the way you live in the world. Recognizing that life is what you make it helps you to write your story from your heart, and not from the worldly activities created by others. You are a creator.

GUIDANCE: "DEVELOP SELF-LOVE & INNER HAPPINESS"

The roleplay self helps us to understand that there is a certain role we play in the world in every aspect of life. This can sometimes take away from who we truly are or our desires for life. We try over and over to make life work and forget that the most important thing is to make sure we work and are enjoying our life's experience. Self-love is important, and when we become more aware of the things that affect our love for ourselves, life can become easier. This is a difficult process for some, because change isn't easy to do.

What I found helpful during my process of change was learning more about myself as a human. This step is critical, because it's the only way to take effective action. We take advantage of our beauty and forget to notice that we are a beautiful creation. Science has developed and provided lots of research on how to improve the human experience. It's not merely enough to live without knowledge of how and why you're living.

While on my journey, I graduated with my Bachelor of Science in Psychology, and it was the best thing for me. Now, this is my personal experience and I don't expect you to go out and learn psychology or get a degree. But what I would like to mention is that during that time, I took a class called "Cognitive Psychology" and it became my favorite topic to discuss.

This class taught me about my brain. It was a topic I had never discussed before, and it changed my life forever.

I will always be grateful to have come across this on my path. I learned how the mind works and was able to understand why I had repeated patterns—repeatedly. It explained why I could not delete bad habits, and most importantly, it helped me to understand why I couldn't change my life.

In order to make any effective change, you must know how. If you want to know how to ride a bike, you must learn right? You learn the process of how to do it and then you get on that bike and practice until you finally get it.

It's crazy, because after understanding this, I could instantly diagnose why things didn't work when I attempted to change before. The lesson I want you to learn from this is to first understand yourself, which includes your mind, body, and soul. Research the mind and how to create effective change. Look for terms like "subconscious mind" and "conscious mind". Effective change starts when you learn what you need to do and how you need to do it.

In order to develop self-love, we must first determine what it means to love ourselves. For me, I had never known that I didn't fully love myself until my first real relationship. I noticed that I tended to make sure everyone else was happy before me. I would put my happiness last on the list and if there was enough left for me, I would take advantage of it. That's not how it supposed to go.

You must learn that the "character" you "play" in this world does not have to determine your life. It should not have the power to determine your level of happiness or self-worth. We put jobs and the amount of money we make before ourselves.

We make careers our priority so much so that we don't even remember to care for ourselves.

Take time to think about what makes you happy. Do material objects, family, friends, activities, or being alone make you happy? Are you allowing your energy to be affected by the roles you play in this world? When you go to work, do your coworkers drive you crazy? Do you think about quitting your job or even your life often because you're stressed?

These are the hard questions you need to ask yourself in order to determine what is affecting your happiness and love of self. Get to the core of the problem. Make assumptions about what may be affecting you, and if it's negative, start to think about ways to make a positive change.

One thing you must take away from this section is that *the roles you play in this world should not determine your happiness*. The things you participate in should not affect you emotionally. The people around you should not have the power to change your mood so easily.

If you are experiencing any of these difficulties my friend, you are allowing your character to write your story instead of your heart. The only thing you need to do in this section is acknowledge that your outside world has affected you in a positive or negative way. This acknowledgment will help with determining what happens next in your life.

Take some time alone and think about all the things that affect you negatively. Write them down. Start to analyze how these problems developed and ask yourself why they affect you today. If you're at a job you don't like, ask yourself why you don't like it. Is it because of the people, the workload, you don't want to work there, or whatever?

Start to have a dialog with yourself in order to understand this person who has subjected themselves to the roles they play in the world. When you understand the reasons why you do things, you can understand how to change them.

EXTRA MOTIVATION JUST FOR YOU!
(NOTES FROM MY PERSONAL JOURNAL)

If I told you my life story, you wouldn't think much of it because there weren't many action plots. My entire life so far hasn't had much action compared to others in the environment I grew up in.

But, that's a different story. We all have our own perspective in life, therefore never tell a person your life was worse than theirs. I was an emotional girl, especially when I was younger. Have you ever had those times when you just didn't understand why you were a certain way?

As I grew into a young adult, I noticed I had more emotional breakdowns that caused me to question my emotional state. For a while, I didn't investigate why I was this way. When you're living life, you don't really take a moment and look at the way you are unless you are psychologically inclined. Which later in life I became after obtaining my bachelor's in psychology. As I went through life, I had my share of mistakes that caused a ripple effect and taught me the lessons I needed to learn.

When I was younger, I didn't have a clue about the "real world" and how difficult it would be to just have a simple, stable life. As I grew older, it became more apparent

41

that this was not going to be an easy process. This is something that also affected many generations before me, therefore I couldn't be mad at anyone for not having the knowledge to make a change.

After starting to learn about the world and its difficulties, I had many questions. How does this game of life work? Must I exhaust myself just to make some money? That's unfair, this can't be true, can it? The crazy part is that's what appears to be true to all those growing up in this lifestyle. Who's going to tell them any different? Then I had an idea, I'll tell them!

While I was writing this, I thought about each one of you who are hurting and can't find a way out. I know the struggle, I know the pain, I know the financial barriers posed against you, but you can overcome. It's important to understand you can be all that you want to be if you believe.

THE PAST, PRESENT, & FUTURE SELF: SETTING

LIFE:

The past, present, and future self is defined as the part of you that determines what moment your thoughts are in. This can be easy to differentiate because it's basically what you are thinking about "at the moment". Are your thoughts about what's happening in the past, right now, or the future?

Self-discipline can be beneficial when attempting to manage your thoughts. Discipline helps you to have more control over the thoughts that come into your mind. You'll want to control your thoughts because you react to them. Developing self-love and inner happiness coincides with having positive thoughts that lead to positive actions. Therefore, it's essential that you know what's happening in your head.

When controlling these thoughts, it's important to focus on the present moment vs. the past or the future. Knowing that our thoughts influence the decisions we make helps us to imagine certain outcomes. Past thoughts can provoke fear or certainty and future thoughts can provoke fear or certainty. However, whether you are thinking of thoughts from the past or future, it's important to make decisions based on the present moment. The past and future are contributors to the decision but should not be the conclusion. What you are experiencing and who you are now is a composite of who you are and were, and where you're going. We can never escape this part of the self. When used in the wrong way, negative/positive thoughts can be detrimental to your life and happiness.

If you were to take a moment out of your day and decide to manage your thoughts for a few minutes, what would you personally experience? You could be constantly thinking about the future, such as goals and aspirations. Or you could always be focusing on the past, such as things you wanted to change or are unhappy about. Either way, not being present in the moment is the wrong setting to be in. **The moment** is where all your happiness is. It allows you to be with whatever you may be experiencing currently.

When I work on my daughter's school work with her, it requires me to be completely present.

She's homeschooled so it's on me to ensure that she learns properly. If I can't focus on what's happening at that moment, I will lose my attention span to assist her. Considering she's in kindergarten, these are the most critical parts of the learning experience for her.

Kindergarteners have a ton of work to do and at times, it can be stressful, especially because my daughter is very hyper. If I allowed stress, negative thoughts, and circumstances to take me away from the moments with her, it could affect her learning. I will admit that if I was as emotional as I used to be, I wouldn't be able to teach her.

Back then, everything affected my present moment. If I had got into a disagreement with someone, the bills, work, and more would change my mood. I would think about what happened in the past over and over. The future bills that were piling up would torment me. All these thoughts affected my current moment. I was lost in all the things that weren't happening anymore.

Now that we have some scope on what this part of the self is identified as, let's dig right into the dirt.

When we are experiencing life circumstances, usually our thoughts are focused on something we experienced in the past, something happening now, or possibly in the future.

Unfortunately, there are horrible side effects that come with this. For instance, we develop trust issues, low or no self-esteem, lack of confidence, fear, worry, confusion, lack of decisiveness, living on autopilot, inconsistency, unhappy, no self-love, and more. The list could go on depending on what moment we are focused on. So, when you focus on a time that's not the present moment, it can sometimes have a negative impact.

This information should provide insight about what is affecting you mentally, physically, and emotionally. Thinking reoccurring thoughts that do not contribute to your life in a positive way should not be allowed.

Understand that these thoughts are only a product of what was implanted in you by yourself or others. Others can only influence you—they can never tell you how to feel or what to think. When you get to a certain age, it's time to accept that your actions cause the consequences, that you receive, whether good or bad. And that your actions can influence the thoughts you think consistently.

You may be thinking, *but what if the thoughts are good?* Well, if your thoughts are good from the past, present, or future, then they won't provoke these symptoms. Positive energy has a way of influencing our bodies in a tremendous way. These symptoms will include self-love, joy, happiness, peace, prosperity, and more.

However, although thinking positive thoughts about the past is better than thinking negative ones, we still aren't present in the moment. When you are present in the moment, it allows you to create new happy moments and build a happier future. These positive past thoughts do contribute to a happier state of mind, but it should only happen occasionally and be controlled.

When I started to notice how my thoughts affected me emotionally, it helped to solve a lot of my unhappiness. I began to monitor my brain, and paid attention to the things and people I reacted to. The way I did this was every time I caught my mind drifting off into a thought, I would catch it. If it was a negative thought, I would notice it, and if it was positive, I would notice it as well. After catching the thought, I would change it to a positive one.

Now this is a step by step process. The first step should be to just notice it instead of acting. What happens is that you begin to open your level of awareness to the brain's processes. If you've done your research about the brain as I suggested in the previous section, you may even know some terminology for what's happening. You are officially ready for the next step thanks to your complete awareness of when your brain starts to drift into these negative thought spells.

After awareness, it's time to act. We can't just be aware we have a problem and not act on it. After I became aware of what was happening in my mind, I started to pay close attention to each thought. If it was negative, I would try to get to the root cause of it. Usually, the root cause was something that happened in the past or some fear about the future.

Therefore, thorough investigation is needed to determine why you're having these crazy thoughts in the first place. *Warning: take this step with caution because you may discover deep rooted hurts and pains that you may have unconsciously blocked.* You may enter a time where you're uncertain what's happening and where you're going with this process, but it's okay.

Unless you have someone there to guide you step by step, there will always be uncertainty. Trust your heart. This is a decision I believe conflicts you most of the time, because you know you're making a good decision. But statistics and other people's opinions tell you different (so just trust your heart). If you're at this stage of wanting to change the way you think, it's because you are tired of the old way of living. Therefore, it's time to start something new, and that may be challenging.

Sometimes, life can become very stressful, and it's because we fail to understand that the problem is due to our lack of brain tuning/life circumstances. So, I want you to understand that if you are stressing about any of the things listed in the role play section, we have a problem. These "worldly" things are what I like to call them. If you remember, it's my favorite term because all these things were created in the world by a person.

They do not compare to the creation of the stars in the sky, the moon, or the sun. Those creations are not worldly and hold such a profound place in my heart. I am spiritual; I believe there is more to me than what happens in this world. My life doesn't have to depend on what happens in the past, present, or future.

When you take control of your thoughts, you take control of your life. The benefits of becoming aware of your thoughts is that you become happier. You are intentionally noticing when you feel bad and begin acting on the process to change those feelings. *I like to say that positive thoughts bring positive energy, which influences positive action that leads to positive results.*

The best decision to make is to stay in the present moment with your thoughts, because you are more aware of your decisions. When you make better decisions, your life becomes what you want it to be. This allows less room for chance and more for certainty.

GUIDANCE: "DEVELOP SELF-LOVE & INNER HAPPINESS"

When you allow yourself to focus on the moment, it helps you to let go of the things that you don't have the power to control *in* that moment. It's also better to understand that the only thing you can control is yourself. Recognize that the only one who can determine whether you will be happy at that moment is you; therefore, accept that **you are the one who has the power**.

There are ways you can self-talk yourself into understanding that your happiness should be primary. You can do this by eliminating some fears, doubts, negative thoughts, and distractions. First, acknowledge what these thoughts and distractions are in order to eliminate them. Keep your thoughts focused on you, be determined, and decide to feel the way you want to feel.

When I started my journey of developing self-love and inner happiness, I had no clue that my thoughts were always visiting the past and the future. It was such a relief to know that I could release those thoughts as soon as they came into my awareness. It was so life-changing. I learned that I didn't have to hold on to my past because it doesn't control my current moment. The thoughts that control the moment are the ones I make right now.

However, it's important to acknowledge the past. The past is what helps to shape our current moments. Therefore, we cannot just throw those thoughts away. They will always exist in your brain's memory bank and be a part of your experience. It's not about eliminating them.

Begin to practice allowing the thoughts that are negative to come and allowing them to go. Like the flow of water. You can do this by paying attention to your feelings. Every day notice when you feel good and when you feel bad. Every time you feel good, make sure you do more things to contribute to that feeling.

For example, when I wake up in the morning, I like to start my day off with gratitude. I say thank you for my home, car, food, family, life, and everything I can think of. This helps to set the mood. Our energy matters and can determine our day. So, when I start my day with positive thoughts, it leads to positive energy, which brings positive situations.

Have you ever noticed when you're in a bad situation, you feel it? You'll start to notice *oh man, this is turning into a bad situation*, and you think maybe you shouldn't have made the decision to participate.

These feelings you have when you're mad, glad, happy, joyful, excited are all part of energy. You can feel them, right? Your feelings are the best way to start with creating effective change. Just start with the simple change of wanting to be happy ALL OF THE TIME or at least most of the time.

With this understanding, it helps to have a starting point. Whenever you're not feeling happy, it's time to start evaluating your thoughts. What were you thinking about that triggered such a negative emotion? If it was a thought from the past, then start to deal with it. Maybe something in the present moment triggered that negative emotion from the past.

First, understand that anything that has happened in the past is over. There is nothing you can do to change it, whether good or bad. This is the first step to acknowledge when you are feeling down.

Also, you cannot predict the future, so don't allow that to control you either. When I started monitoring my thoughts, I noticed how most of them were based on past events and future events. When the thoughts were negative, it would hurt me all over again. It felt like I was living the moment again.

After having these thoughts, I would then associate them with my future, and it would make that worse too. I wasn't living in the present moment at all. Or my present moment was stolen from other moments.

When a negative thought appears, just notice it and don't attempt to build a story around it. For example, you're sitting down watching a TV show and something happens during the program that triggers an emotion in you. While watching the show, you suddenly feel sad in your heart.

Now your experience has changed, and you don't know why. Your current moment is now one of negative feelings. If you ever encounter this type of situation, first acknowledge that you aren't happy for some reason. Next, think about what you just did or what just happened.

In this scenario, you just watched a TV show and was triggered. So, you take a moment and think about the thoughts that ran through your head. It was that time when you experienced the same negative situation you saw on TV. You had a memory of it, and it made you relive the moment with your thoughts. The brain communicates with the body to remind you of how you felt when that happened.

Certain triggers can affect our frame of thinking. Our thoughts can change from positive to negative in an instant. You can begin feeling sad unconsciously if you are not aware of these processes. There are things happening all around us to be cautious about. Protect your energy by fighting to stay in the moment.

Accept the truth that you are no longer living in past tense and can't determine future predictions. When you take each of these actions, it will teach you how to let go of things easier. You will no longer have these negative thoughts clouding your brain and controlling your every decision.

When you let go, it brings you to a place of peace on the inside. This peace helps contribute to your happiness. Happiness brings so much joy to your heart that you are left with no choice but to love life and yourself.

EXTRA MOTIVATION JUST FOR YOU!
(NOTES FROM MY PERSONAL JOURNAL)

I need you to*

I know it may feel that every day is hard, but I need you to believe in easier days. I need you to do this because I sincerely care for each one of you reading this book. The reason it may seem hard now is because the odds are against you in your mind, but I need you to let those odds go.

When I finally overcame my emotional problem, it was like a weight lifted from me, and I began to live life again. I had never really known all that time I was living my life on autopilot controlled by emotions. It's called the subconscious mind, and it's powerful.

The negative emotions had a tight grip on me and didn't want to let go. At this point, they weren't going to let go of me, so I had to let go of them. The great part about this life is that we have a choice, but we make ourselves believe we don't. If I could ask a favor, it's for you to feel my positive energy as you read this, because I need you to understand _you have a choice_! Since you are provided with an option, how about you choose life? Especially because it's already short enough.

Now, you must begin to be aware of the things that may be holding you back, and one by one—attack them! We all have something in life that may be hindering us from a great future, but I need you to act now for positive change. Take this book and let it be the beginning of something new. There are so many resources for you to learn from, so let this be the start of a brand new you.

Motivation

Every day, I strive to be the best I can be. Sometimes it may be hard, but no matter what I pull through. Challenges will come and go, but I must remain the same— "at peace". Don't beat yourself up when you don't do your best. You must consciously feel better and take control of your thoughts. Acknowledge the momentum when you're in a great place.

Change

Change starts with a decision and ends with consistency. You need to realize the fight you're up against such as: neurons in the brain, a lifetime of habits, and the inability to change effectively. It's so easy to revert to what we are used to. But is that the best decision?

Things to realize: Some people have changed, some people may not want to change, some people may want to change but are unsure how, some people know they need to change but don't care enough to, some people think they've changed but haven't, and some people are in the process of change. What category are you in?

OUTER SELF: PLOT

LIFE:

The *Outer Self* is defined as the part of you that is how you are viewed to others. The only difference between the OUTER SELF and CHARACTER is that the *OUTER SELF* is how you look at yourself. It is not about how the world sees you or the role you play. It's solely based on your perception of yourself.

This is the personality, ego, and all the other self-defining matters. We think of ourselves in a certain way, and this perspective of who we are in this world is critical. It affects our decisions, self-love, and happiness. Mainly, because we can choose to view ourselves from the perspective of others or we can choose to view ourselves in our own way.

Imagine that you have a lack of self-confidence and maybe you've put on some weight. You hang around some new people and they acknowledge your weight gain, and it makes you feel a lack of self-confidence. This has affected your self-image, and the way you view yourself. Now, there is a thought that you are overweight and must do something about it because of what another person has said.

You are now self-conscious about everything you wear, the places you go, and how you look. You've never took the time to accept your image and create your own perception of how you look.

This feeling of lack of confidence now affects your happiness and self-love, because you are putting conditions on yourself. You now view yourself compared to many others that may be a different size, which is either one size too big or one size too small. Having this lack of self-confidence has now changed your entire perspective of yourself. Viewing your life from this perspective can be very dangerous and inconsistent with your peace and joy.

This is because you cannot live a balanced life when you are viewing yourself from the image of others. In life, every individual has their own view on things, and it should never be compared to other's view. What I'm saying is that we can only view things from a selfish perspective, and this means we can only view things from a perspective of self.

If we can only view things from our own life experiences and self, then we should be very careful when putting someone else's opinion above our own. This is not to say don't take considerations from others or value them. It doesn't mean being selfish. But it's more important for you to put your opinion first.

My own self-image wasn't something I thought about too deeply. I didn't know the value of my own self-worth and that I needed to care about how I feel about myself. As I went through my life journey, I started to notice that certain things about me changed. When I got into a relationship and had different stresses, my appearance changed. When I started businesses, my perspective on what others thought about me changed. It's just been a journey of inconsistent love for me.

Self-love wasn't something that was critical to me because I didn't even think about it. I was last on my own list. My image was built based on who others thought I was, or what I thought I should be in the world. I thought I should graduate from high school, go to college, get a job, and everything else. This was implanted in me. It wasn't technically who I was or what I wanted. It was more about what I had to do or what I thought I had to do.

This routine became my outer image of myself. It's who I thought I needed to be for the world. We can easily forget who we want to be when there is so much conditioning in the world. There are commercials that promote what you should do in life. Your parents are always telling you what you should do. All of this suddenly becomes your life, and you think it's what you must live up to.

Okay, it isn't that simple, but it's real. What you subject yourself to is what influences your perspective on life. If you watch TV shows that promote a certain lifestyle, you could become interested in that way of living. If you hang around a certain group of people, you'll begin to think that you should act a certain way. What surrounds you daily could become how you view your life and the outcome.

Ask yourself questions in order to begin the process of determining how you view yourself. You can ask questions like: What makes me happy? What do I love about myself? What is my purpose in the world? How do I feel about others? Do I care what people think? And so on. Start to interrogate yourself so you can have an idea of how you feel about the way you are. When you begin to think about your outer perspective on life, then you can see yourself the way you've always thought you to be.

I remember when I started to ask myself these questions, I noticed a lot of things about myself that I didn't particularly like. But then I realized they were traits that I had picked up along my journey of self-discovery. I didn't want my self-image to be what I had become, because I felt it wasn't me. I felt I was viewed as someone who was always ready to argue, mean, stressed, and all the things I don't believe about myself. I didn't want to view myself that way. I wanted to see myself as a caring, kind, patient, sincere, and a genuine person. Therefore, I had to eliminate the traits that I noticed made me the negative version of my OUTER SELF.

Of course, other people can help you with determining your Outer Self. But I do not want this to be confused with making other people's opinion matter over yours. Instead, they can help you as you transition to the next phase of self-growth. We need the assistance of other people along our journey.

If you know someone who genuinely cares about you, then you can communicate with them. They can let you know how they view you from an outer perspective. When you get this criticism, you should only consider it and not allow it to become your main reason for change. Take the information into consideration that the other person has provided and compare with how you view yourself. If it is similar and you agree, then make the appropriate observations.

If you don't agree with their opinion of you, then simply dismiss if from your thoughts. You can do this by being understanding that the other person has the right to view anything how they want. Also, understand that every person will view life from their own perspective because that is the only way we can operate. You do not have to base your decisions on what others think of you. Thank them for their honesty and continue with your process of evaluating yourself.

Now that you've taken the necessary steps of evaluating yourself, getting feedback, and adjusting your decisions, you can begin to make some changes. How do you want to view yourself? Begin to write down the things you want to change. There are multiple ways to make the change effectively. Research some of the best options in order to assure your results are beneficial.

For example, if you decide that you no longer want to be emotional, then you can research "how to deal with emotions". The internet has a lot of resources to help. Choose what best fits your time frame and lifestyle. Personally, I utilize mediation, which includes listening to brainwave music for about 30 minutes daily. During the meditation session, I sit still, close my eyes, observe the thoughts that come, let those thoughts go, and continue to relax myself.

Meditation helped take me to a place of comfort. It provided me with the outlet I needed when I felt I had nowhere to go when my emotions got tough. It showed me how to effectively breathe in and out, and how to calm down. I learned that just because I had this outer experience happening to me, I didn't need to have a full mental breakdown.

I also learned that the way I view myself is important. And not to put myself last on the list. The goals I set would help me by becoming the person I've always sought out to be. That kind, caring, loving, sweet, and genuine person was starting to become my outer image. With my new understanding, I was able to view myself differently, which allowed me to accept myself.

GUIDANCE: "DEVELOP SELF-LOVE & INNER HAPPINESS"

In order to develop an outer self that you are pleased with, you must put yourself first. The best way to learn how to put yourself first is to stay true to your heart. When you stay true to yourself, it is the most simplistic way of staying in alignment with your goals and inspirations in life. To do this, think about what makes you happy. When I thought about what made me happy, it was feeling completely at peace with all things in life.

I didn't want to care what other people thought about me or work at jobs that no longer fit my positive vibes. It is important for you to take a moment and access what makes you happy in this lifetime, because this will be the motivation to keep going in the hard times when you are in the process of change. And there will be hard times.

I must address all the distractions that are put in front of us from the mass of society. These distractions prevent you from having a life created by yourself. All the TV commercials, shows, ads, social media, and more are promoting some way of how you should live your life. Whether you realize it or not, it shapes your perspective of your own life. Over time, we develop an image of ourselves that we didn't intend to have. Help yourself by beginning to eliminate some of the distractions in your outer world. Don't go on social media as often, don't watch negative TV shows, spend your time around positive people, and dedicate time for you.

Every day wake up with the attitude that "I love me no matter what happens". Understand that positive energy brings more positive situations. You might be in such a negative situation that it may be hard to think of yourself differently. If you're experiencing such a difficult time, it's not going to help by making yourself feel worse about it.

Don't judge yourself for every little mistake that you make. I noticed that often I would be so critical of who I was that I didn't even like me. It didn't feel good that I couldn't be who I wanted to see myself as. When I learned how to stop judging myself, it made life easier.

Most of the time, we learn to judge ourselves by listening to what others think of us. We take their opinions about our lives and make them facts. When they have become facts in your mind, it's hard to understand facts from fiction. Say someone tells you "you're controlling" and you hear that all the time. Sooner or later, you start to believe you're controlling. Now, every time you act or deal with another individual, you must address whether you're being a control freak or not.

All these ideas get in your head and start to become your outer perspective of the identity you carry. Eliminate the ones you don't agree with. People are always going to judge you and view you how they want. You do not have to do the same to yourself.

The process of eliminating those judgements is to first acknowledge what thoughts these are, for example, if you view yourself as controlling. When you acknowledge the judgement, ask yourself whether you truly believe you are controlling. If you believe that sometimes you are unfair to others, then you can practice communicating more effectively.

This can include listening to others when they speak or simply asking them their preference in whatever the situation may be. This allows you to relinquish some of the control and give the other person the same ability. Now you are becoming whole, because you've accepted a flaw within and chosen a path to take to fix it.

EXTRA MOTIVATION JUST FOR YOU!
(NOTES FROM MY PERSONAL JOURNAL)

Positive or Negative

I see myself past the struggle, past the pain, and past the hurt. What I'm going through right now is all a test, all a game, and a question of my strength. At times, I ask myself "So, what will it be positive or negative?" The negative thoughts like to creep up on you and destroy everything you have, and they will try to break you down to your last bone. But you must know that thoughts can't, and you can shift consciousness.

There is and will only ever be positive or negative. When I ask the question "positive or negative?", what would you choose? This phase in life is important because this is a decision you must make, and it's critical not to be conflicted with the decision.

*What's your purpose? *

So many people on earth are unsure of their purpose in life, so their time here can be difficult. Purpose means the reason for which something is done, created, or exists. Every person has a purpose, whether they believe it not.

There is something we should all be doing, and that could be something such as being happy. The happiness that radiates from you could inspire and touch others. You can't allow all other situations to become the focus of your life instead of what makes you happy.

INNER SELF: CONFLICT

LIFE:

The **Inner Self** is the part of you that lives within, like a spirit or soul. It is normally the most conflicted part of life. We have a voice inside our heads that we consider the thoughts from our brain, and we never seem to question it. We think thoughts daily and conflict with decisions on what to say or what to wear. This is the part of self that is very powerful, and it's sometimes difficult to understand from a worldview perspective.

Now, this may be a touchy subject if you don't believe there is a part of you that is not physical. The reason for writing this book is to speak about the things I have discovered. Therefore, I would be dishonest with you if I didn't tell you that I believe we have a soul/spirit that lives inside our bodies. I wouldn't be happy with myself and therefore conflicted as well. I must stay true to my beliefs and share them as I believe my purpose is to do so.

We are beautiful creations in the human world, and the most critical element is the soul/spirit within. What is the soul or spirit, and are they the same thing you ask? Well, the soul and spirit are the same thing in my book, but it's important to use both terms because you may have a different perspective. The soul/spirit is the part of you that is not physical. It lives within while you're alive and lives after the body dies. Sometimes I think of it as pure consciousness.

During my youth, I encountered many experiences that led me to believe there is another part of me that lives on past this body. After all my experiences and research, I concluded that I am energy and everything that lives is energy. The body is a vessel that helps my soul/spirit live this life experience on earth.

There are so many spectacular creations that make me question my own human self. Think about it… can you create the moon, stars, sun, clouds, or any of that? Something that's not a someone created these beautiful creations and created me. My body is special in every way with every breathe it takes. It takes me on a journey every night I sleep and every morning I wake. There is something unique happening thanks to this creator of the universe. Therefore, I refuse to believe that after I die, there is no me.

Listen, I'm not trying to convince you to change your belief system because it's of course your choice. There are many different religions and cultures who have different belief systems, and I'm not trying to change that. But what is true is most people accept that something exists outside what we can see and experience.

What I do want to do is get on the same page about the fact that there is more to you than this body, these life experiences, and everything you can think of. For example, maybe you've experienced *déjà vu*. When something happens that you KNOW or BELIEVE you have experienced before. When déjà vu appears in my life, I am just astonished. It's something I just can't explain.

In my own life, I have seen things happen in the craziest ways, and they could have never happened normally. These occurrences happened so many times that I cannot reject what I know and believe to be true. Which is that there is more to this world than what we think and it's time to rise and accept this.

I think it can be a very scary process to go through, but why fear life when we are going to die anyway? One premise I live on is that life is short, and you never know when it's your time. You have no control over who your parents are or when or how you will die. We cannot avoid birth or death because it's something that will happen no matter what. If you have this understanding, it's important to treat every day as special just because you woke up.

Of course, it's normal to ignore your spirit when everything around you seems so real. Why believe in something you've never seen? Before I started to think about my spiritual self, I was more focused on how to live normally "in the world" and fit in with other people.

At one point in life, I was associated with Christianity, but it was only because the people around me were. I was young. I knew the basics of the religion, but nothing more than that. Although I had this religion, I didn't feel connected to the true source or whoever GOD was. If I wasn't connected to God, how could I connect to some spirit in me?

All these questions would race through my mind as I went through life. As I grew, a big part of me became my spirit, and it is to this day the most dominant force about me. The main reason we either seek, run, or consume ourselves in topics of this sort is because there is something deep within us that is connected to it. Before I obtained my Bachelor of Science in Psychology, I was just a girl with a dream running around clueless. I was a Christian praying to a God in the sky that I don't even know whether I believed in.

Studying psychology helped me to learn about how the brain functions. I learned about the brain and how it works, which helped me to understand my human body. We discussed topics such as neuro pathways, conscious, subconsciousness, and more. It was so helpful to understand what was happening within my body. But none of that really helped me understand that voice inside my head, or the deep emotions that came along with it.

After I soaked up all the psychology for the moment, I still felt there was more. That my mind didn't have the control I thought it did. There was something guiding my mind, because in my opinion the mind is just a computer program that does what you program by learned behaviors.

At this point, I had to learn more about myself and the world I live in. Research helped me extremely. I learned about the universe and how the scientist studies our bodies. There was an overload of information that forced me to accept my truth of knowing that there is more to this human body than I know. There was always a feeling inside of me that knew there was more to life.

Yet for some reason, I lacked faith that the soul/spirit within was real. But it was only because I didn't have a true understanding of life or who I was. There are so many assumptions made on what happens after death. There are even NDE (near death experiences) that people talk about. These are stories from people who say they died and came back to life. During their death process, they encountered a spirit-like form of themselves without a body.

These stories don't have to convince you about believing you have a soul/spirit. The main purpose is to inform you that inside you lives someone special and if you dig deep enough, you will discover the trueness of it. On the other hand, not knowing yourself fully can affect your overall perception of your earthly experience. You can find this inner person in several ways.

When you go to sleep at night, there is a part of you that is awake in your dreams. For me, I was able to sense my spirit/soul when I meditated. After I closed my eyes and practiced breathing, my body became still. In the stillness, I would feel a presence within me that wasn't physical. The way I felt it was as if there was someone else inside me, and a deeper part to me.

I also would stare in the mirror at myself directly in the eyes for about 5 minutes. After a while, I would feel awkward because there was a part of me that was looking at the person in the mirror. As if I wasn't the person in the mirror. I wanted to congratulate the person in the mirror and tell her I would always be there for her. You could try these methods yourself and see whether you encounter a feeling or presence that you've never felt before.

GUIDANCE: "DEVELOP SELF-LOVE & INNER HAPPINESS"

D on't feel pressure to decide whether you have a soul/spirit right now. My goal is not to force or confuse you. However, I do have to be honest with you. I lived life without fully connecting to my spiritual part of me for a long time and I was miserable. And I've lived life since then completely understanding the spiritual part of me. This experience has changed my life drastically.

I talk about psychology a lot and how learning about the mind has helped me. However, my journey has been 30% knowledge about psychology and 70% finding out that I am connected to the source that created this beautiful world, which absolutely astonishes me. I fell deeply in love with myself because I know that there is more to me than a career, money, and everyday life!

I want you to feel this good too. I sincerely do. You never have to feel weak, damaged, or any negative emotions, because you are connected spiritually to the source that created the world. You're loved genuinely.

This can be a lot to take in, so just understand that you are more than the body you wake up in every day. And that makes you powerful. Your repetitive daily plans and actions are just a part of the journey of discovery of your true self. When you find out this information, I hope you just fall madly in love with yourself. Flaws and all.

Self-love starts with knowing who you are. This knowing of who you are helps you to connect fully with yourself. And there is no better connection than the one with the self. Self-love brings peace, love, joy, and happiness into your life. Once you have submerged yourself with this feeling, you can't help but to radiate happiness. Loving yourself literally changes your life. It eliminates the walls and barriers that held you back and silences the voices of things that aren't good for you. Doesn't that sound good?

To start this process, doing research about your mind, body, and soul/spirit should be a critical part of your journey. You can't change if you are unsure how. Considering every person is different, this book cannot guide you on YOUR path. Only you can. You know the specifics about yourself.

If you have decided that there is more to you and you have a spirit/soul connection, then there are limitless possibilities for your experience. You have the entire universe, family, and friends to help you make things work in your life.

If you have no clue about where to start on this spiritual journey and want to believe there is more to you, then start with your heart. Your heart is the closest feeling to what your spirit feels like. It is sincere, genuine, passionate, and more. When you make decisions from this place, it has a profound effect on your happiness. You open the doors of limitless possibilities and get to work with the same source that brings out the sun every morning.

Imagine having the same source you trust to bring out the sun, moon, and stars on your side. How powerful? Aren't you just as unique as them? If you don't think so, then it's time to change that mindset to knowing that you are special because you are a part of the universe and loved.

Practice getting into the mental space that brings peace by doing something you love. For instance, meditation allows you to quiet your mind. It helps you to be in the present moment and accept life for what it currently is. When you meditate and stay in a still place for some time without moving your body, you will begin to feel a sensation that is different from the physical self.

Maybe this practice can help you connect to your soul/spirit. Exercise is also a good way to lift your spirits because it promotes good health. It allows your body to feel healthy, and that brings positive energy.

EXTRA MOTIVATION JUST FOR YOU!
(NOTES FROM MY PERSONAL JOURNAL)

Beauty Within*

When will we realize the love is within, and that we were uniquely created to be special beings? Before we entered this body, we knew who we were on a spiritual level. So often people don't value their greatness and that is because they are focused only on their weaknesses.

What would happen if everyone in the world learned that we are all special and loved? The world would be beautiful, but is it really a dream to a have a beautiful world?

Why do people have to teach pain and suffering? Well, unfortunately that's just the way the world was taught to grow together.

Who am I to judge? It took most of my life to get it right, and I'm still learning. Life isn't always easy when you don't know how to live. Most of this happens because we aren't taught, we are just talked at. With all this knowledge being acquired and understanding of one's self, why not share the wisdom? When we share, then everyone can experience the beauty within themselves.

*Who am I? *

You enjoy the journey because the "end result" doesn't matter. There is no "end result" because life is ever flowing. How comforting is it to know that there is no need to stress about the "what if's"? The wholeness of who I am is being exposed in all ways and I'm not afraid.

Why? Why am I not afraid? There is no hiding from the thought that I may be more than this body, there is no hiding from the thought that I may be more than what the world thinks of me.

*Meta*Meditation*

(Discussion with self) Breathe in and breathe out. Relax, relax, don't be controlled by your mind; you have the power. Do you believe you have the power? Tell me please!! It's important to believe. Focus, focus, focus!!! Breathe in and breathe out. Relax, relax.

*I find meditation a helpful tool for clearing out the mind and being in the present moment. If you don't like to meditate, there are other ways to become more present such as exercising. The goal is to allow yourself that time to relax and be one with you. You become more aware of the thoughts that may have been affecting you, and you notice why things in your life are the way they are.

The battle of yourself

It is very important to acknowledge that throughout life, the only person we are battling is ourselves. It can be easy to blame others and look outside of ourselves for problems. One must have wisdom and accept the fact that "I" am responsible for the decisions I make and the outcomes of my life.

There are a few steps you can take to come into this acceptance. Those steps include becoming more self-aware and facing reality. When you are self-aware, you can be in the moment more often, and notice what you are going through within. Facing reality helps us to take off the mask we so often put on in situations. Whether you are afraid of the outcome or just do not want to face it, you must.

. *In this moment meditation*

(Discussion with self) (Brainwave music playing)

I am all I can be in this moment of bliss and total awareness. My greatest potential is right in front of me. All the hurt and the pain subsides. I am guided in all my ways and expect great results from my actions. Every day is a great day, and this is the truth. There is a greatness within you, and you must walk in this daily. Don't allow the worldly struggle to become your life. How long have you been in despair? It's time for some happiness!

I need you to be joyful no matter how hard life gets. Delete those fears of failure because they have no power over you. Understand that you have this great wisdom inside you that must be displayed to the world. We become our thoughts, so think great of yourself.

IN BETWEEN- SELF: THEME

LIFE:

Your life always has a theme from which you base all your decisions. Our beliefs tell us what decisions we should make. It either helps build our confidence or knocks it down. In this book, the perspective we are viewing is the theme of your faith. Faith is believing in the unseen or unknown.

Faith doesn't always have to be associated with a religion or higher power, because you can have faith in yourself. It could be faith that you will accomplish all your goals, and that your strength is enough. Future events aren't always promised to go the exact way you think they should. That's when we incorporate faith into our lives. We want to believe that what we don't see happening or helping can happen.

The In-between Self is the part of you that is always going back and forth about your faith and life decisions in general. This section is like the inner-self section, because it discusses spirituality, but the main topic is about your faith. You may believe in God, the universe, Jesus, Buddha, or yourself.

The IN-BETWEEN SELF discusses how you are in-between what you believe and what you don't believe. It's alright—this can happen to anyone, but you do need to accept where you are with this part of you. Acceptance is key to evolving into your happiness. This section is important, especially because in order to develop true happiness, we must be whole, which means knowing and understanding every part of ourselves.

I was once fully lost in the IN-BETWEEN self. I thought I had faith in whoever God was, and that I was truly happy with myself. God was this mystery, and I didn't fully understand. Your belief in the practice you service affects your life tremendously.

Let's use one religion as an example, such as Christianity. This is my personal experience with this religion. My intentions are not to offend with the example provided—they're just for illustration.

When you are a Christian, there are certain rules you must follow in order to be part of that congregation. If you don't follow those rules, there could be consequences. When you are a part of this religion, there is a specific idea of the person you must be. You must act a certain way and attend church sessions a certain amount of times a week.

This is a big commitment especially if you have full-time house duties like kids, family, and work. This could put a strain on you mentally, physically, and emotionally. But you continue to go through with the process as if it's a requirement for your life.

Because this religion of Christianity is your culture, it becomes your life. It controls the way you eat, think, speak, and more. You follow the orders, even if it means disregarding your own happiness. Sometimes you don't fully understand why you're participating other than it may benefit your life. There is a part of you that can't escape because you know you must obey. You are always living two different lives: one for the church and one for home.

Although you're going to church, things are still the same at home. You listen to the preacher week in and week out, but still no changes. Frustrated, you can't seem to understand why you're unhappy and do not love yourself or your life.

This is only one scenario, because you may be extremely happy about your Christianity. It may have helped you to become the person you are today, and life may be great. If this is true for your life, then I am extremely happy for you. Overall, the goal is to develop self-love and inner happiness.

I congratulate all those who found their way in life through religion and have also helped others. We all experience life from different angles. But what I've learned is that only *you* can make you happy. There is not a religion, a person, a car, a house, or money that can satisfy the hunger your body needs of LOVE. That is, self-love.

Decisions are what help us to grow. Decide that you are going to put 100% faith in the practice you follow. But only decide that if it teaches you how to love yourself and become truly happy within. Sometimes religion can force decisions on our lives that we don't necessarily agree with. This causes conflict between you and you.

Part of you wants to participate and the other part wants to be free. There are good parts of religion that teach you how to develop these techniques, but then there are others that attempt to control you. At the beginning of this book, there is scripture from the bible, Matthew 5:14-16. This is placed in the book not because I'm a religious person. It's because of the message it has delivered and the impact it has made on my life. It helped me to understand who I am and gave meaning to my life. It provided the understanding that I am the light of the world, which means that I can change the world by first changing myself. It motivated me to become the best version of myself, which meant to heal from all my wounds and grow so that I can show others how to as well.

Before, I wanted to hide from the world because I felt it was so crazy. And the message I received from this scripture was that I can't hide because the world needs me. We don't become better to keep the techniques to ourselves. We become better to share the love with everybody else.

What messages are you getting from the life that you are living and how is it helping you become the best you?

GUIDANCE: "DEVELOP SELF-LOVE & INNER HAPPINESS"

The best thing I can say is *keep it simple*. No matter what religion you are part of, the most important thing in life should be your happiness. You should never have to feel or act a certain way because of any type of rules. Especially if this rule is affecting the way you feel about your life.

Yes, it can be hard to approach life when there is a belief you hold about it all. What I would like for you to do is step away from the titles, the positions, the reputations, the money, the experiments, the religions, the people, the drama, the popularity, and ask yourself: what's left?

When you answer that question, you should be able to say the love for myself. I love myself so strongly that no one or nothing can take me away from me. I am extremely happy and all the things in the world cannot take it away. This should be a ritual or religion. Let's make self-love a class, because if we all truly cared deeply for ourselves, the world would be more positive.

If you are part of a religion, then be sure to stand your ground about your beliefs. Do not go back and forth about whether you have faith— make a solid decision. When you decide to have faith, it ignites your trust in the source you believe in. Throughout life, you will have this certainty of knowing you are not alone and there's help. Your trust will be like knowing the sun will come up. Having this consistent faith helps you to go through difficult and good times with a smile.

One example I like to use is that the sun, moon, and stars are always playing their roles. They never let us down. You won't wake up one day and the sun is missing because it has given up on lighting up your day. No. You have faith and belief that it will be there shining.

Have you ever thought about that? The sun won't disappoint you. It may burn you, but it will never leave you. If it did not play its role, then you would be shocked.

Can you understand that whatever source created this beautiful world created you? And that source seems to never fail with the other duties.

The flowers are fed, and the stars are shining. In my opinion, the only difference between you and a star is that you have free will. The stars don't have that option; they must obey the laws set for them.

When you accept that there is more to you than your body, you open yourself up to endless possibilities. You can develop a new faith that maybe there can be something more than what this world can offer.

It can be scary to think that our lives are in the hands of the world. Especially with all the crazy things happening. Psychology helps us to understand that it is our instinct to attempt to connect to a higher power. This is usually why people join a congregation of religion.

Releasing any conflicts with the overall theme of your life will help you make better decisions. It will provide clarity in your heart and life. Choose what you will believe for your life.

In my own personal life, I no longer have a religion. I believe in the universe, and spiritual guidance. I believe I am a part of all that is and that all things work out for my good. This is my faith. In the past, I thought being a Christian was my life until I completely evaluated whether it benefitted me.

When I prayed, I was not connected to the source that created the world. I would hope that maybe I could get help based on my behavior. This was conditional love, and I would hear stories that God gave unconditional love. I didn't feel like this was what I received.

I thought I had to be perfect and always ask to be forgiven of my sins. What I learned is that in order to know what love is and how it feels, I had to love me. The process of religion didn't work in my life because I didn't understand myself. Faith can't be initiated if you don't understand what it is.

After I understood that I had to love myself first, it helped me with knowing I am loved from whoever the higher power is. This is when I learned the power of faith. Before I thought I had faith, but you can't have faith one moment, then the next you don't. You either believe or you don't.

I decided that it was better for me to believe in a higher power. The one that created the world, and

I didn't have to think how the religion wanted me to. The God/source/universe that loves me is truly unconditional. This was life-changing and shifting. Therefore, decide what you will believe and stick to it. Don't allow the different views and perspectives of the world to conflict with what your heart knows and accepts to be true.

Developing self-love is deciding to put you first. If you can't love yourself, you can't love another. If your faith has caused you to live a certain life and affected you, it's time to make some adjustments.

EXTRA MOTIVATION JUST FOR YOU!
(NOTES FROM MY PERSONAL JOURNAL)

Higher Power*

So often, we build this wall that becomes our way of living, but what happens is the wall limits your life. Life is meant to be lived and lived is what it should be. How often do we ponder in the shadows of the dark looking for the light? We should know the light is deep within us the entire time.

Life caused us to ask and we cause ourselves not to receive. This simple fact is because we don't realize that our receiving comes from another place not of the world. When will we accept that the world, we live in is created by a higher power?

This higher power helps individuals be creative and bring into this world creations such as houses, cars, and whatever we want! Everyone is made special and unique, so why search for anything on the out-world instead of the in-world? Love is there if you only allow it in. Sometimes we don't see what's right in front of us, and that's because our brains are clouded with thoughts of struggle.

We struggle to live this thing called life on our own. When will we realize that we are not on our own despite what happens, our beliefs are just that, "our beliefs"? What are you going to do today to be the best you?

A conversation with God/creator/universe

ME: *I'm feeling sad right now.*

GOD: **You shouldn't because I love you.**

ME: *I know but it's just hard to accept what's going on.*

GOD: **You must let go, you're holding on to something so tight that you can't control daughter, why??**

ME: *I don't know why father??*

GOD: **I know why, because you're not thinking of me child. I told you I love you and to trust me. Everything you're feeling right now is by choice. Everything will work out, but I need you to be prepared.**

ME: *I hear you father but I'm still having a hard time not being hurt.*

GOD: **Daughter, I urge you to let go____. that space you're in right now is not your home. You have a home with me. You can't hold on so tight. I need you to be strong for me. Do you hear me?**

ME: *Yes, I do.*

ORIGINATED SELF: RESOLUTION

LIFE:

D o you agree that who we are today is a creation of everything that we have experienced on our life's path? In every moment, you are a unique individual who is set out to do great things and live a beautiful life. The role you play in this world impacts your outer and inner self, and the theme of your life places you in-between who you are and what you believe. While we are experiencing all these different parts of life, something is being developed and created. That something is special and can't be hidden, and that is you. I couldn't wait to talk to you about this "Originated Self" you're making.

Every part of the path that you take contributes to the next moment, and every moment is special. As you live in these different versions of yourself, what's happening can seem overwhelming and confusing.

As we're playing our role in life and shifting through the changes we often experience with family and friends, we forget that we are creating someone. That person is being made from all the intricacies that make you who you are.

The Originated Self is the created version of everything that you are. It's what you have programmed yourself to be from all your experiences. From start to finish. It's who you are, and you can't fake it.

It's the part of you that is glowing with love, peace, and happiness despite anything you've experienced. There's no running from this part of self because it is you, and where ever you run it will follow. It's with you at birth and all the way until death. It's the you that emerges into this world with a specific purpose, and who is ready to tackle any challenge that comes your way. It's the you that conquers the world and makes it through all the hard times. It's the you that wakes up every day, and even though it may be hard it's the you that pushes through.

Never feel bad about anything you have experienced in life because it has helped your journey. Life is a journey. It's not always about who gets there faster or who wins. It's about the little moments that make you smile when you're down. And the times you helped someone in need because they were hurting. But most importantly, it's about the process of you becoming the person you are meant to be.

Only you can provide the answer for your life. Only you can feel the emotion from all the things you've been through. You are unique my friend, and don't you ever think different. Who are you at this very moment and how do you feel about your life? Your answer should be self-uplifting and inspiring. We are not born to live a devastating life that we're unhappy about.

Start to use the different parts of you to become the whole version of you. I remember exactly when my life started changing because it was transformational. I was tired of the same way of life. It didn't feel like it was the life I was meant to live. I wasn't living for me, and the decisions I made didn't make me happy.

I was afraid that if I started to become who I was on the inside, that my life would change. Part of me knew it would change for the good. But change has the power to put fear in you, especially if you've never done it before. I didn't know what the path would lead to if I started to love myself. It didn't even appear to be real from the perspective I was living at. All I knew is that I wasn't happy with the life I was living at that time.

THE FINAL ACT (GUIDANCE: DEVELOP SELF-LOVE & INNER HAPPINESS)

A t this point, I think you have discovered a lot of valuable tools in order to implement change. Not just any change but effective change. Understanding the elements in this book of the different parts of self is beneficial. It's beneficial because it allows us to evaluate every single part of the self and determine where we need help.

The goal of this book is to help you develop self-love and inner happiness. From this moment forward, understand that you should and must love you first. Learn the strategies and techniques of how to become happy and loving to yourself. Once you have developed this inside you, it will shine like a light. You won't have to work hard to help others because they will be so happy to be around you.

You will become this creative person who puts their all into everything giving it life. And the world will notice it and love you completely. You don't need love when you are love. Become so full of yourself that you burst with joy, peace, and happiness. Although I can't go around the world and spread my love to those who hurt, I can utilize the platforms that are already created. I will let my light shine and hopefully brighten up someone else's day. Will you?

There will come a time that you will pause and look at your life for all its worth. You will question your decisions and ponder on your journey. Every moment will be filled with the decisions you made up until this point.

When you reach this point in life if you haven't already, won't it feel good to say you gave it your best try? Knowing that in every moment you were conscious enough to decide what's best for you or not. Having great memories that bring joy instead of pain. I know that I am so grateful every day for the journey I am on, and how it's played out.

I remember the days when I was sad and the days when I was glad. I remember the changes and stages of growth. I see the future ahead and I'm living in the current moment. There is no place like peace of mind. Having the consistent knowing that no matter what I go through in life I will love myself and be happy about it.

There will always be decisions we make that maybe weren't the right one. But what the heck, have fun as you do. Understand that life is about the journey and the result will be whatever it'll be. Accept your flaws and learn your truths.

You are on a path that's going to take you many places. Places you've never imagined. You better enjoy the ride. Self-love and inner happiness provide this feeling that brings joy and peace. They make you want to wake up every day happy and spread the love.

It's the feeling of letting go of all the negative things and people that aren't good for you. It's the feeling of saying my happiness matters so I won't answer that call that'll make me mad. Or the feeling that says I won't eat this unhealthy food that'll drain my energy.

Self-love is deciding that I am who I am and there's no one else like me so I better be the best me. It's understanding every part of yourself because you care.

Take advantage of the knowledge that you have learned today. Understand that in life sometimes we must play characters and must be the ROLEPLAY self. Accept that our thoughts can take us on a journey without us moving with our PAST, PRESENT, AND FUTURE SELF. Keep that self-image in check with thinking the grandest thoughts about yourself managing your OUTER SELF. And please don't conflict with your INNER SELF any longer, because there is something so beautiful about you deep within. With all these parts of the self-controlled, there will be no need for an IN-BETWEEN self. Do all this and I promise you will love your ***ORIGINATED SELF***.

Be proud of your *Originated Self* because there's no one else like you. After everything you've been through, you still push through and try to make life better for you and those around you. There's not much guidance needed in this section because the only true guidance is within you. I know you know what to do next!

EXTRA MOTIVATION JUST FOR YOU!
(NOTES FROM MY PERSONAL JOURNAL)

Alignment

You are not controlled by outside forces, you are a spiritual being. Always keep this in mind, especially when you're dealing with the societal world. I know sometimes it can be difficult, but you must stay in alignment with who you are. It's time for your life to change for the good. You have come so far, and I can guarantee that it is your time. There will be no going back. Every second will be dedicated to becoming all you need to be!

Strength

I believe that life can at times be difficult for all people of every age, color, financial class, and more. There will always be challenges and difficulties that people will experience. The main lesson to learn from these experiences is to gain strength to move forward from your mistakes. Growth is a key essential in life, and it can help you become your greatest version of yourself.

Having strength is pushing through when times get tough and you think about giving up. The proper mindset should be

121

you can, and you will. We all need to take advantage of the strengths within us. Without this realization, how can we live the most effective life? If you understand and accept that this is not an easy process, you can then be prepared at every moment.

Gratitude AFFIRMATIONS

- *I am so happy and grateful now that my husband and I have manifested consistent income.*

- *I am so happy and grateful now that with the money, we have bought our new house, cars, blessed family and friends, and live a wealthy life.*

- *I am so happy and grateful now that I have gained wisdom and knowledge that will forever be in my mind, body, and soul.*

- *I am so happy and grateful that I am at my weight goal of 116 pounds, and completely healthy.*

- *I am happy and grateful now that every day of my life will be beautiful despite anything that attempts to interrupt me.*

- *I am so happy and grateful now that I am in full control of my life and living in the spiritual world, not the physical world.*

Affirmations are a good way to train the mind of repetition to new thoughts. Think of some things you would like to see come true in your life and repeat them daily.

LOVE FLOWING

Love, love, love, it's all we ever seek.

Why didn't anyone teach me I don't have to live the worldly version of me?

Knowing what I know, my life is now for sure different.

I have no clue what happens next, but my spirit has my back and that's the truth.

This universal presence that's so undeniably true feeds me daily even when I don't realize, it will still do.

My heart seeks this calling, and I do believe, but never choose to step out and achieve.

Why, why, why? So long we suffer in the misery thinking woah is me.

You are loved more than you can imagine.

On a ship, on a boat, or in a cabin.

There is nowhere love doesn't flow. Eliminate all the worldly thoughts and you'll know.

It's within you and everything you see.

When will you truly believe?

The time is here.

The moment you called upon the real journey and the real path.

Consciousness, trust, it will always last!

ABOUT THE AUTHOR

S hantinique James was born on November 19, 1991 in Detroit, Michigan. Originated Self "How to Develop Self-Love and Inner Happiness" is her first inspirational self-help book created to inspire readers. Shantinique holds a Bachelor of Science in Psychology and is currently working on her Master's in Psychology with plans to obtain her PhD in Psychology.

She has worked with companies in the Medical field in her working life. In September 2016, she started her movement called "Nique's Life Worth Living Movement" dedicated to helping people find their inner self to develop love and happiness. She plans to continue to write books, do motivational speaking, and counsel individuals. Shantinique is the mother of two beautiful daughters Maliya and Ayla. In life, she will inspire millions of people looking to better themselves.